WHAT OTHERS ARE SAYING
ABOUT THIS BOOK:

Be Silly (signature)

" Yvonne Conte is like the conscience I never had.
Holding this book is like holding the hands of a Healer.
It should be prescribed reading because, unlike most
medications, it actually works. If Richard Lewis ever
read this book, his career would be over. "

Chris Rich, Comedian/Writer,
"The View" and "Comedy Central."

" Bits of Joy is a charming reminder that the little
things in life are still the best. So buy it, open it up and
commit to an idea a day. It could turn your life around. "

Janette Barber, Supervising Producer and
Head Writer, "The Rosie O'Donnell Show" and
author of Best seller, "Breaking the Rules, Last Ditch
Tactics to Landing the Man of Your Dreams."

" In today's fast paced high stress corporate
world we all need a bit of joy! Open up this adorable book,
take a breath, collect your thoughts and feed your
soul with a spirit of Joy! "

- John Gabriel, Telecommunications Consultant,
Atlanta, GA

Bits

of

Joy

150 Ideas That Will Make You Jump For Joy

Yvonne Conte

Illustrations by Anna Cerullo and Yvonne Conte

Amsterdam-Berwick Publishing

YVONNE CONTE

Bits of Joy
150 Ideas That Will Make You Jump For Joy

By Yvonne Conte

Published by: Amsterdam Berwick Publishing
                  PMB #231
                  4736 Onondaga Blvd.
                  Syracuse, NY 13219

Ordering Information:
Individual sales: All Amsterdam–Berwick Books are available through
                      most bookstores. They may also be ordered on line at:
                      http://www.crack-a-smile.com and *www.amazon.com*

Quantity Discounts: Purchases used as college textbooks and or client gifts
                    may qualify for special discounts and are available to bulk
                    purchasers by contacting:

**Special Sales Department
Crack-A-Smile Seminars
PMB #231
4736 Onondaga Blvd.
Syracuse, NY 13219
(888) BE-SILLY**

Printed in the United States of America
10 9 8 7 6 5 4 3 2 1

First Edition
Library of Congress Cataloging-in-Publication Data

Conte, Yvonne 2003

Bits Of Joy
Joy, Happiness, Self Realization, Family, Workplace Humor

ISBN # 0-9665336-4-X

TABLE OF CONTENTS

ACKNOWLEDGMENTS

Gratitude first and foremost, to my Lord for all the blessings He has given me. To my children, Aubry and Johnny for their never ending gift of love and unwavering support. To my dear Mom for giving me life and teaching me that laughter is a powerful gift. To my sisters Donna, Jacky and Annie for fifty plus years of warm hugs and wet your pants giggles.

Thank you to David Rose and *4allthingsweb.com* in Chattanooga, Tennessee who looked at the Fun Free Tips section on our web page and said, "Why don't you have this in a book?" Thank you David for the idea to write this book and for creating a web page that actually works!

Thank you to sister Donnarae Bryne for her unrelenting support and never-ending belief in me. You are my cheerleader, my champion and my hero. You get the prize for being the absolute funniest person who ever walked the earth – yep, funnier than Lucy.

Much gratitude goes to Terri Zbick for her personal coaching and uncanny ability to motivate me to actually sit down and write. Thank you for teaching me how to concentrate on one thing at a time, for listening to all my nutty ideas and for being a faithful sister.

Thank you to cousin Carla Jonquil for her editing ability and invaluable advice - also, for giving me that great recipe for scones. Thank you to John Viglucci for his patience and kindness and for his ability to come up with ways to make my thoughts look so good on paper. Much credit and love to Anna Cerullo whose whimsical sketches captured visually what I have tried to say here in words and for her natural ability to be a sweetheart.

A thunderous applause goes out to all the people in my audiences. Thank you to the companies and organizations across the country that so graciously have shared with me their fun filled anecdotes and silly ideas.

To my hilarious friends; Tonja Bernard, Carolyn Williams, Barbara Holbrook, Albert Pylinski, Terri Zbick, and John Gabriel for making my sides hurt. You are the people I have laughed the hardest with and I am eternally grateful.

Bless you each and everyone for your support and love and for the JOY you are to me.

INTRODUCTION

Joy may come from the coo of a newborn baby, the smell of fresh coffee or having a friendship with your Lord. However, the sprit of joy is a way of life. It is an attitude about life. Joy is taking every opportunity to experience love, to be grateful for each day and to savor each moment. Living a life of joy comes from within. A truly joyful life is available to anyone who is willing to take the time to pursue it.

Nationally sought after Motivational Humorist, Yvonne Conte shares 150 activities that have continued to add joy to her life. This book combines joyful ideas with the whimsical drawings of her friend, Anna Cerullo in the hope they will help add joy to your own life journey. Bits of Joy is an extension of the commitment at Crack-A-Smile Seminars to helping others live a joyful life. This manual is full of ideas that are certain to add laughter, joy and creativity to your day.

"Happiness cannot be traveled to, owned, earned, worn or consumed. Happiness is the spiritual experience of living every minute with love, grace, and gratitude."

--*Denis Waitley*

BEST WAY TO UTILIZE THIS BOOK

Bits of Joy may be used as a resource book, a daily idea book or a simple guide to fun and joy. It is for everyone who is seeking a joy-filled life. This book is designed so it may be opened to any page to reveal something interesting to do.

Organized into five sections, this book will provide joyful activities to do with the children in your life, with your family and loved ones, during your work day, to inspire you and to bring you joy. Some activities may be perfect for you and others may seem just plain silly. Be courageous. Try all the activities that give you a chuckle. In many cases the one you hesitate to try will be the most meaningful for you.

We hope that you will take advantage of the ideas in htis book to further your quest for a joy-filled life. We invite you to share with us any additional ideas that have brought you joy.

CHAPTER ONE

Bring in the Joy

Silly Ideas to Get You Started

"The unselfish effort to
bring cheer to others will
be the beginning of a happier
life for ourselves."
— Helen Keller

We donate at the office, we put money in the basket on Sunday, we walk three miles for MDA and we buy Girl Scout cookies. When we share our time and our talents to make other people's lives better we are truly giving. In this chapter you will find ways to give, be grateful and add to your joy filled life. So dance with abandon, sing out loud, smile at a stranger, be kind for no reason or buy yourself a gift. You will find more joy than you imagined. Most of the ideas in this chapter cost little or nothing and take only a few moments of your time. Be generous with yourself and others. Treat your life like the gift it is and see what a difference it makes.

"He will yet fill your mouth with laughter and your lips with shouts of joy."
Job 8:21

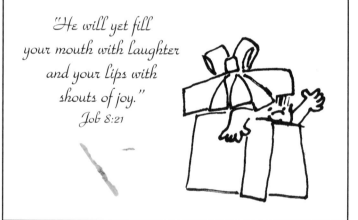

BE A VOLUNTEER

If you really want to feel great, volunteer. If you know something that needs attention go ahead and offer your services or just show up at a friends house and say, "Today I am here for two hours to do whatever needs doing. I can clean the garage or basement, shovel snow, plant a garden, vacuum, do the laundry or baby-sit. Where do I start?" Your help will be a remembered moment of joy for someone else. By offering to spend time to help someone you are giving a surprisingly wonderful gift.

BALLOONS FOR NO REASON

Just a few brightly colored balloons can change the atmosphere in any room. It does not have to be a special occasion to enjoy them. Bring a balloon to work or better yet take a few home to your spouse. Give a great big balloon to a stranger for no reason at all. Balloons make a person smile and can brighten up an otherwise ordinary day. Balloons say party and parties are fun! Go out and have yourself a balloon filled day.

JOKE FILE

Keep an envelope near your desk or in a kitchen drawer. When you see something funny, silly or interesting clip it and drop it into the envelope. Clip jokes, cartoons, or any item you think may be of interest to someone you know. Once a month sit down and mail the items to friends and family with a quick note letting them know you were thinking of them. People love to get 'real mail'. In fact they open real mail first! Your thoughtfulness will be a welcome change.

PAY IT FORWARD

Do something wonderful for someone without them knowing that you did it. Tell no one and wait and see what wonderful thing happens to you. You may have seen the movie, 'Pay It Forward'. It is a wonderful drama about a young boy who tries to change the world by doing good deeds for people without them knowing he did. The idea is that each good deed makes someone else's life better. Soon the recipient of the kindness would 'pay it forward' by doing a good deed for someone else. Pay it forward. Nothing brings you more joy than bringing joy to someone else.

BE GRATEFUL

Find a quiet place. Each day find a moment while you are doing dishes or walking to your car. Close your eyes and breathe deeply. Think about your blessings for a moment. Either write them down or make a mental note. Who are the family, friends and co-workers that you are most grateful for? What places or things are you thankful for? Are you grateful for your health, career, education or your personality? Take the time to say a thank you to your maker for all the gifts you have been given.

LEARN SOMETHING NEW

Do something today that you have never done before. Try something new. Your brain needs exercise as much as your legs and arms. By learning new things each day you keep life interesting and fun. It can be something simple like learning a new word or more involved like learning to rock climb. Make it a goal to do something new and different each day.

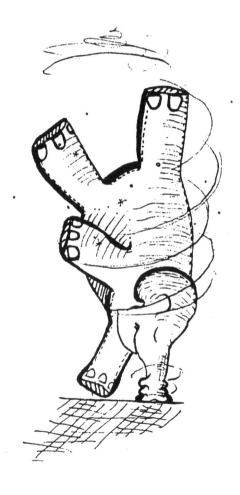

CAN You hear Me Now?

TELEPHONE SOMEONE SPECIAL

Sometimes we get so busy with our work and families that we tend to forget those people in our lives who are alone. Make a list of the people you know who live alone. It could be an aunt or uncle, a grandparent or a college student. This Sunday surprise them with an unexpected phone call. Tell them you wanted them to know that you were thinking of them. Ask about their day. Ask a young person what their future plans are. Ask an older person to tell you stories from the past. This is a simple but effective way to bring a little bit of joy into someone else's life.

LEARN TO DANCE

Learn a new dance. Try a dance you have always wished you could do like the Tango, the Twist or the Jerk. Have you ever danced the Macarena? Join a dance class, rent an instructional video or just ask a friend to teach you a few steps. Just hearing music will lift your spirits. Go ahead and dance a little - you don't even need a partner. Dance in the living room or in the backyard. It is wonderful exercise and is sure to put you in a groovy mood.

RELATIONSHIP SPA

Even the best of relationships can get stale at times. We are so busy with life we forget to take an extra moment to nurture the most important part of life, the relationships we have with our significant other. Set aside a day or a weekend when the two of you can be completely alone. Make a plan to simply have fun with each other. This fun could include a walk in the woods holding hands or a bubble bath. Try this once and you are likely to make it part of your routine. Remember to add laughing together to your spa day.

JOY LIST

Striving to live a balanced life seems to be on everyone's agenda. But how do we do it? Start by making a Joy List. Think of all the things that add joy to your life. The smell of fresh coffee, a crisp fall day, a child's smile, a job completed and lunch with your best friend can all go on your Joy List. If it makes you happy, it goes on your joy List. Then make a commitment to engage in a few of these joyful things every day. Count your blessings every day. This list will become a priceless tool for days when you are feeling a little down and out. Choose five things that have brought you joy in the past and allow them to bring you joy today. Living a joy filled life is a choice we make. Choosing well will bring balance to our lives.

SMILE!

Our mental outlook is determined in part by the expressions we make. Researchers have found that when we turn the corners of our mouths up even if only to hold a pen between our teeth our mood improves. If we can improve our mood just by smiling, can you imagine what a good, hardy laugh would do - or a wink? Try it. Wink at your sweetheart. Smile at someone you know and laugh really hard with the person you love most.

GROCERY STORE

Sometimes a trip to the grocery store can leave you feeling like you have run a marathon. Everyone is in a hurry. A quick, easy way to be reminded to slow down and enjoy the day is to give away a smile. A simple smile is sunshine to the soul and the countersign of friendship. Set a goal the next time you are at the grocery store. Do not leave until you have made at least five people smile.

CARD PARTY

The next time you feel a little low go to your nearest card store and read the funny cards. Some of them are so hysterical you may feel like showing them to the shopper next to you. You do not have to buy any but you may find one you just cannot leave behind.

SHINE ALL YOUR SHOES

My father had a wooden shoe-shine box with a place for the shoe on top. Inside were soft cloths, a brush with black bristles and lots of pots of polish. I loved taking his worn shoes and making them like new again. I've got Dad's shoe-shine box now and I use it to keep my shoes looking great. A person looks so much better with clean shinny shoes. Footware lasts longer when taken care of, but the best benefit is the feeling of accomplishment when you see all your shoes looking great. You will make a better impression with good-looking shoes. Shine your shoes. It is a quick and easy way to put your best foot forward!

TRAFFIC JAM FUN

There is nothing fun about getting stuck in a traffic jam. Or is there? Instead of getting stressed out, reach into your glove compartment and pull out a clown nose. The next time you are stuck in traffic put on your red sponge clown nose and wait for the person next to you to notice you. Watch the fun begin and the stress end. See how many people you can get to laugh before the traffic resumes. While you are having fun passing the time you are helping those around you enjoy a moment of laughter. Grin your way to work.

MAKE A SNOW ANGEL

Did you ever make snow angels as a child? Remember how much fun it was to lay in the cold snow and stretch out as far as you could with your arms and legs and move the snow into the shape of an angel? Put on old clothes, go out in the snow and make a snow angel. Ask a friend to join you. It does not matter how old you are. The more you do the things you did as a child the more fun you will have in your life today.

ACT LIKE A HERO

Carol Burnett, Lucy, Jerry Lewis, Jim Carrey, Woody Allen, and Bill Cosby. These are my heroes. They filled their lives and everyone else's with laughter and fun. I want to be like them. I read their books and watch their movies and keep their pictures around to remind me to always look for the lighter side of life and keep my world filled with joy. We grow into that with which we admire. Choose your heroes carefully. Study them. Put up their pictures. Emulate them and let their lives inspire you.

BE JOYFUL

When Roberto Benigni accepted his Oscar for the movie, "Life is Beautiful", he was so full of excitement and overjoyed with happiness. He said, "This is a moment of joy and I want to kiss everybody because you are the makers of the joy!" He was expressing to all of us just how incredibly happy he was. By expressing that joy to us he became even happier. When you express your emotions it intensifies them. The next time something good happens to you, express yourself. Tell all your friends and family how you feel. Sharing the good news will make you even happier.

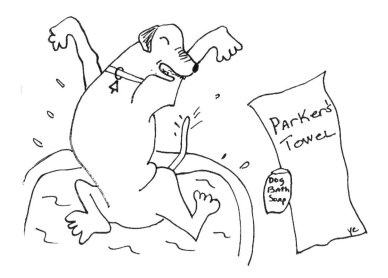

DOG BATH

Give your dog a bath and make it the most fun you have had all day. Use silly toys or a fragrant shampoo. Blow-dry the hair and add ribbons or a great bandana. Tell your dog you are getting him or her ready for a big date and then take the dog for a walk in the park so everyone can see what a beautiful pooch you have.

THE ART OF LETTER WRITING

Before computers, calling plans and cell phones people wrote letters. They were works of art – full of funny anecdotes about the children and a laundry list of all that was going on. Letter writing has become a lost art. I have an aunt in Pennsylvania who has no computer, no calling plan or cell phone. Once a month I write newsy letters to her and I am always excited when I see one of her pretty envelopes in my mailbox. Take the time to write someone a letter. Get nice notepaper, pretty envelopes or stickers and take your time. Brew a cup of tea and sit by the fire as you write. Oh, now that is a joy.

WATCH COMEDY SHOWS ON TV/CABLE

The act of laughing has been said to make you a happier person. So what makes you laugh? Do you like I Love Lucy, the Three Stooges, Dick Van Dyke or older sitcoms? Do you prefer Seinfeld or Comedy Central? What makes you laugh? Is it slapstick? Do certain facial expressions crack you up? Are there any particular words or phrases that send you into a belly laugh? Collect tapes of your favorite comedy and keep them handy. You never know when you will need an invigorating chuckle.

CHEER BOOK

Create a "Cheer Book" for someone going through an especially difficult time. Fill a small, plastic photo album with special pictures of loved ones. Include a group shot of everyone wearing clown noses. Add individual photos using funny props. Nothing works better than a smile when life does not seem to be going well.

SING A HAPPY SONG

Do people sing because they are happy? Or are people happy because they sing? Philosopher William James said, "If you act enthusiastic, you will be enthusiastic!" I think that goes for all of the emotions. You can fake it till you make it! If you want to be happy, act happy. If singing makes you feel good, find the happiest song you know and sing it with enthusiasm. I guarantee you will start to feel happy. Best of all you will be in complete control of how you feel.

BUY A FEATHER BOA

If you do not have a feather boa it may be time to get one. Wrapping yourself in feathers can turn an otherwise dull day into an amazing adventure. Make a list of ten interesting and fun things you and your husband or kids can do with a feather boa. Just making the list can be an entertaining evening. Then follow through and turn each idea into ten more fun and eventful evenings.

THE GOOD THING ABOUT BAD NEWS

There is so much bad news in our world today that a person could become very depressed just by watching the six o'clock news. One way to turn depression into impression is to think about something bad in the world and then think, "What is the one thing I can do to make that a little better? Put your idea to work. Do something positive. If each of us did one thing to make the worlds problems better, think what may happen.

VISIT A SMALL TOWN

Spend this Saturday vacationing in a small town. Choose one you have never been to before. Find a local coffee shop or mom and pop grocery store, put on a smile, walk in and ask the oldest person there to tell you about the town. Ask about the buildings, the town hall, the cemetery and the best place to eat. There are lots of small towns and villages all over America that have much to offer. You may see a beautiful Appaloosa horse farm or find a wonderful antique shop. You'll be surprised at the joy you discover in your own backyard.

BE CURIOUS

My father used to say that in order to be interesting, we must be interested. Take a genuine interest in another person and see where that takes you. By asking someone about his life you may learn something new. This is a great way to connect with people and make them feel important.

LET EVERYONE GO AHEAD OF YOU.

This quick and easy idea will lift your spirits. When you are waiting in line at the lottery machine, at the grocery store, the post office or driving in your car, let some go ahead of you. Do it with a smile. It costs you nothing. It makes both of you happy. If you're at the lottery machine, who knows - it may even bring you some good luck. Doing something for someone else is a sure way to make your day a bit more joyful.

KNITTING LESS STRESS

Knitting seems to be the stress buster of choice for the Hollywood and New York actress set. My daughter Aubry uses knitting to fill the time she spends waiting during rehearsals and behind the scenes during stage productions and she is not alone. Tyne Daly, Cameron Diaz, Daryl Hannah, Hilary Swank and Julia Roberts all carry knitting needles with them where ever they go. Tyne Daly says, "It relieves tension and stress and fills the waiting time." She calls it her Irish Meditation. Knitting can settle the spirit and give you quiet time with yourself. You do not have to be an actress to use this joyful form of relaxation. The bonus can be a great sweater or night-cap!

GO ON RETREAT

Create your own retreat. Decide what it is you would like to do. Do you want to sing, read, dance, paint your toenails, do some gardening? Set aside some time for your retreat. If you have a week to go on your retreat, great! If you have only an hour, use that hour for your retreat. Remember this is your time.

JUNK PARTY

Have you ever had a community garage sale and ended up buying your friend's stuff while she bought yours? That is because one man's junk is another man's fortune. Have a party and invite your friends to bring a few things with them that they no longer want or need. Your guests may take home with them as many treasures as they brought to the party. This is a wonderful way to recycle useful things you no longer have a need for and a great reason to visit with your friends.

ADD HUMOR TO YOUR LIFE

Laughter and humor are good for our mental and physical health. The quickest and easiest way to add humor to your life is to surround yourself with people who make you laugh. Spend time with the funniest guy in your neighborhood Make friends with the wackiest person at work. Go to funny movies. Write comical letters. Send amusing gifts. Call your silliest friend and giggle. You really can add more fun to your life. It is a choice you make.

YOU CREATE HAPPINESS

Take a good look at the word REACTION. If you mix up the letters you come up with the word CREATION. Both words have the same exact letters in them however they have totally different meanings. People are like this too. Some people REACT to what happens around them while others CREATE what happens to them. We can react to traffic, to the kids, to the teapot whistle and life just sort of goes on. Or we can choose to create a specific life for ourselves. We can decide to create a happy, more fulfilling life. We have a choice. When negative things happen, as they often do, you make the decision as to how you will react. Create your happy future.

BE FULL OF CHEER

Brighten someone's day by bringing him or her some cheer. Call someone and sing a song. Ask a friend to go for a walk. Read a joyful story to someone who is sick. Bring someone a flower. Mark Twain said, "The best way to cheer yourself is to cheer somebody else up."

HUMOROBICS

Most of us need to exercise more often. To make it more fun, try Humorobics. Hop around on one foot and pat your head while reciting the words to an old nursery rhyme. Then try changing the words to the rhyme to make it more interesting. Put your hands on your hips, twist at the waist and recite the names of the last five restaurants you have visited. This is a surefire way to wake you up on a dull day.

PLAY DATE

Set aside time each week to have a play date. This is especially important at times when you feel you have no time to spare. That is when you need a play date the most. Connect with one of your children, a friend or your significant other. Use the swings at the park, skip around the block or have a bike race. Let the child in you escape and do not let anything get in your way.

VISIT COMEDY CLUBS

For a great time and a major stress buster go visit the nearest comedy club. You can call ahead and ask to be notified when clean comics come into town. Some comedians can be very naughty, so you may want to avoid the 'blue' nights. While you are there notice the things you laugh at the most. Try to fill your life with more of that kind of humor.

TAKE A PILL

Multi-colored candy such as M&M's can be your best stress relief. Put them in small bottles labeled for each ailment. Assign a color to different stressful situations. Red can be when you are red-hot mad, yellow when you are full of fear, and a brown when you are down in the dumps. Green can be when you over worked. Take an M&M as if it were just the pill you needed. Having this silly stash of stress busters keeps the humor in your day. The candy may be a tasty treat but it is the humor that actually reduces the stress level.

MIRACLE STORY

Read about a miracle. Find a book or story about some amazing event. When you read about astounding, wonderful things that have happened to other people it helps you realize that miracles really do happen and they can happen to you.

FUNNY PEOPLE

The best way to turn a bad day around is to spend some time with a good-natured friend. One day I took a friend of mine to a wonderful tearoom where tiny sandwiches are served on a silver tray. I took one look at the tiny sandwiches and said, "If we ate like this everyday we'd be thin." My friend replied, "If we ate like this everyday this tray would have teeth marks on it!" Some people see humor everywhere. That 's the kind of person to spend time with regularly.

GET OUT YOUR HIGH SCHOOL YEARBOOK

What did you look like in high school? Better yet what did your boyfriend or girlfriend look like? Take that yearbook off of the shelf, dust it off and have a good laugh. It is good to look back at the past and see how far you have come. It is even better when the past gives you a good laugh.

LAUGHING FOR THE HEALTH OF IT!

Laugh out loud. Right now – just bend over and hold onto your tummy. If you do not have a tummy, hold on to the person next to you and laugh as hard as you can. Ha Ha Ha Ho Ho Te He!! Doesn't that feel good? Laughter is a great way to massage the muscles around your heart and lungs. It brings fresh oxygen to your brain. And it is just plain fun!

COMEDY CLASS

Read books by, for and about comedians. They will teach you something about the comic mind. Some of these books will be just plain funny. Most will also teach priceless lessons about what makes us laugh and how to find more laughter in our lives. Keep a joke book handy. Anytime you need a break open to any page and enjoy a chuckle.

CHAPTER TWO

Whistle While You Work

Ideas to Infuse the Work Environment with a Spirit of Fun

"If I couldn't laugh
I couldn't stand this job
for fifteen minutes."
-President Abraham Lincoln

I have traveled all over this great country promoting work time laughter. From Fortune 500 corporations to little mom and pop shops, people are putting on their clown noses and standing up for their right to actually enjoy the workplace. It is no secret that we are much more productive when we are happy at work. On the following pages is a collection of ideas to get you started on a quest for silliness at the office. It is time to infuse your work environment with the spirit of fun.

"A merry heart doeth good like a medicine: but a broken spirit drieth the bones."
Proverbs 17:22

PROMOTING FUN AT WORK

Promoting fun at work creates closer work relationships, makes a job more attractive and can reduce turnover. It is easy to add more fun to your workday. You can be the Director of Fun and appoint someone Vice President in Charge of Humor. Create silly contests – the person with the most sales for the week gets a free lunch. Put humorous sayings on the bulletin board – "when you get to the end of your rope tie a knot and hold on". Organize a volleyball game or card game during the lunch hour. When you enjoy your time at the office, it is a much better atmosphere to work in. You will see a big difference in company morale and a rise in productivity.

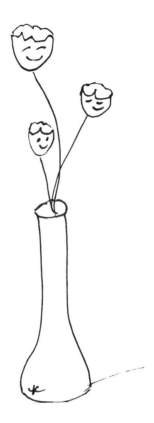

UNEXPECTED GIFTS

For no reason at all do something fun for someone at the office today. One of my co-workers once put a small vase with a rosebud on my desk with a note that said, "This Buds for you!" Pop up some popcorn and drop it off at a friend's desk with a note that says, " I'm feeling a little corny today." Stop and pick up some candy to take to someone special. Add a note that says, "Just for you sweetie." Unexpected gifts will bring joy to someone's day and will make you feel good for having provided that joy.

COMPLAINT TANK

We often work with people who are quick to whine and complain about things but never come up with ideas to make things any better. There is a way to turn complaints into solutions. Create a complaint tank. Have co-workers put all their complaints in the tank and at the Monday morning meeting break into groups. Have each group take one complaint. Make this a contest to see which group can come up with the best solution to a problem. Everyone becomes part of the solution. Empowerment is a powerful tool.

GIVE YOURSELF A FUNNY FACE BREAK

Look into a mirror and make a face at yourself. Now keep going until you make yourself actually laugh. The sillier you are the better. Taking five minutes out of your day to be completely silly is a great way to rejuvenate yourself so you can get back to work refreshed and ready to be productive.

TAKE A TRIP TO THE TOY STORE

It is amazing how quickly your childlike personality returns when you walk the scattered aisles of a toy store. Spend some time looking for items to lighten up your home or office. With a coloring book and crayons you can enjoy a coloring break. Find some toys to take back to the office that are filled with bright happy colors or just make you laugh to look at them. You may not be able to buy happiness but you can buy things that make you smile, giggle and remember how to have fun. The toy store is full of them.

EASTER EGG SURPRISE

The Executive Vice President of Weight Watchers Canada shares this great idea. Fill a fishbowl with your employee's names. Ask your executive office staff to pick a name from the fishbowl. Then type a note to that person telling them something special or something they really admire about him or her. Put the note inside a plastic Easter egg and secretly place the egg on that person's desk at some point during the week before Easter. This is a wonderful, fun thing to do. Everyone feels good to be appreciated.

PAGING SILLINESS

The workday can drag on and on sometimes. What you may need is a boost of laughter to revitalize everyone and get people moving again. Pick up the paging system and in your own voice, page yourself. Everyone will wonder what is going on. Or page a famous person to get everyone's attention. "Oprah Winfrey. You have a call on line one. Oprah Winfrey line one."

FEWER MUSCLES TO LAUGH

It takes fewer muscles to laugh then it does to frown. A good hearty laugh positively affects fifteen major organs in your body. Researchers say that three minutes of good, hard belly laughter is equal to twenty minutes of strenuous rowing. Belly laughter stretches the muscles from the diaphragm all the way up to the scalp. That stretch releases the tension that causes fatigue, stress and headaches. Do whatever it takes to add a little laughter to your workday.

PASS THE IDEA ON

When someone comes up with something fun to do at work make a note of it and pass it on to another department, vendor or client. Create a "funny stuff to do log" complete with pictures of your department enjoying the day. Share what works and change this world one smile at a time.

LAUGHIN' ON HOLD

Keep a small joke book near the phone. The next time you are stuck on hold instead of getting frustrated with the wait. Take a humor break instead.

APPRECIATION

We are much more productive people when we feel appreciated. It is so easy to let someone know that you appreciate his or her work. A simple thank you makes a world of difference. If there is someone in your office that makes your life easier - tell him or her and give an "appreciation award" – perhaps a lollipop or a stick of licorice.

BAD HAIR DAY

Having a bad hair day? Wear a silly headband. No one will notice your hair. They may be too busy laughing. Do you need to feel like a King or Queen? Wear a crown. Wear something silly on top of your head and give your co-workers the joy of a good belly laugh.

TAKE A NEW ROUTE TO THE OFFICE

There is something to be said about consistency, but every now and then it is good to break the mold. Just for the heck of it go the long way to work, stop at a new coffee shop, eat your lunch with chopsticks or open the mail with your opposite hand. In other words do something different. The change of pace will be good for you. Keeping your day full of surprises is a great way to make every day new, interesting and fun.

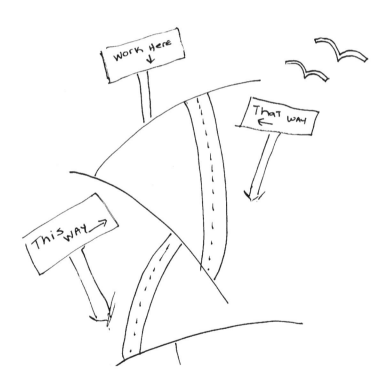

STANDING OVATION

Give someone a standing ovation today just for coming in to work! This is a fun opportunity to let someone know they are appreciated.

BULLETIN BOARD CONTEST

Ask co-workers to bring in a picture of themselves as children and post them on the bulletin board. During the day people can try to match the baby picture with the right co-worker. Give a prize (a toy of course) to the first person to correctly identify the pictures.

HUMOR FIRST AID KIT

When you find yourself so frustrated with a task that you simply cannot think straight...it is time for a break. Reach for your Humor First Aid Kit, a small box filled with anything that is guaranteed to make you laugh. Personalize your kit with cartoons, funny pictures or whatever makes you smile. The purpose of the kit is to distract you for a moment. It helps you relax enough so that when you do get back to the job at hand you will be ready to focus and be productive.

SUNRISE SILLINESS

Find the funniest morning radio show in your town. Tune in and start your day with a few good chuckles. If the morning crew is not your cup of tea, collect the CD's or tapes of your favorite comedians. Listen to them during your morning commute. There is no better way to start the day then with really good humor.

MINI VACATION

Some offices have casual days. Once a week you get to wear casual clothes to work. I call that a mini vacation - a nice change of pace. You look different and you feel different for that one-day. Take it a step further and you are sure to get a chuckle, a giggle or at least a grin. When you are having fun, the day just goes by faster and easier. Think up a fun mini vacation for your office and watch the smiles. Schedule a clown nose day (everyone wears a red foam clown nose), - a silly hat day (everyone wears a silly hat), a 70's day (everyone wears polyester), or an Elvis Day (everyone comes in bloated!)

HUMOR LIBRARY

Start a humor library at your workplace. Stock the library with your favorite comedian's tapes and books. Encourage others to do the same. Sample different types of humor by using this library for a humor break instead of taking a coffee break. Laughing together is a great way to build strong work relationships.

INVENT GAMES

The next time you are faced with mountains of work or are about to get all stressed out over a problem that needs attention, decide to make it fun. Make a top ten list of ways to solve your problem. Time your tasks to see which ones you get done fastest. Turning your work into a game will make it fun and when your having fun you get more done.

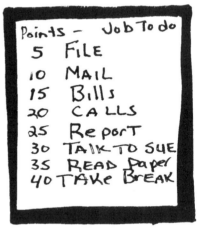

Points — Job To do
5 FiLE
10 MAiL
15 Bills
20 CALLS
25 Report
30 TALK TO SUE
35 READ paper
40 TAKe Break

ASK FOR HELP

Are you the kind of person who has always done everything yourself? Does it seem easier and quicker than asking for help? Have you ever thought that this might not be the best way to do things? Asking for help is something that every happy person knows how to do. Make a point of asking for help with something once a day – and then let the person follow through with your request. Do not worry; you will get better at this with practice. When you ask someone for help you are saying that you value his or her advice, experience and knowledge. By working together you create a bond. Do not be concerned about repaying the people who help you or keeping track of who has helped you. Simply be a person who offers help to others and accept their help in return.

BE COLOMBO

If you want to be an interesting person you have to be interested in other people. When you meet new people think of the experience as your Colombo game. Colombo, the investigator, was always asking questions. Try to ask as many questions as possible about a new acquaintance. Try to find the person's passions. People love to talk about themselves and will be eager to offer all kinds of interesting information about their life. In the business world the more you know about others, the more successful you will be. Knowledge is everything. Be curious and genuinely interested in others.

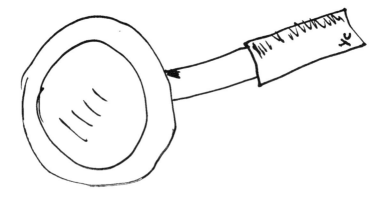

FRIDAY AFTERNOON OFF

Create a Friday afternoon off contest at your workplace.
Set up a contest centered on productivity goals, positive
suggestions or the special needs of your workplace. The
winner gets Friday afternoon off with pay! This is a great
way to motivate people and get them to think creatively.

LUNCHTIME WITH THE UNITONES

This idea comes from Linda at Unisys in Farmington, NY. She tells us Unisys employees who moonlight as musicians have organized a company band, The Unitones. When the management team at Unisys cooks hot dogs and hamburgers for the 300 employees they are backed up by their company band. Company fun encourages a happy, cohesive workplace. Is there a company band lurking at your workplace?

IT'S IN THE CARDS

When you feel the cards are stacked against you, change decks! You can find a variety of motivational, inspirational or just plain funny cards to brighten your day. It is time to stack the cards in your favor.

MANAGEMENT CAR WASH

Here is another great idea from Unisys. The management team holds a car wash once a year and the proceeds go to the employee events committee. Seeing the management team working together creates a positive atmosphere for everyone. This is a great way to increase company moral while putting some cash in the bucket for more fun filled events.

LUNCHTIME GYM

Invest in a volleyball net or a basketball hoop for your office parking lot. You may also want get the soft sponge type games for the break room. Being able to work off some steam by playing sports in the middle of the day can be a smart stress reliever. Playing with your co-workers during breaks and lunch hour creates a more cooperative atmosphere during work time.

THE DALE CARNEGIE MEETING STARTER

Most sales people dread the Monday morning sales meeting. Whatever you did not accomplish the week before gets talked about in front of the team and if you are not the number one sales person it can be a very demoralizing experience. Many years ago I worked for The Dale Carnegie Institute as a sales person. We started our meeting on a high note by having each person tell the person to their right, something positive about that person's work. It may have been how they handled a phone call or a networking situation. It may have been a letter they wrote or a client they were able to secure. The benefit here is threefold. We started the meeting feeling like winners. Our peers appreciated us. We learned from each other's successes. I loved it.

Childish Ideas

Activities to do with the Children

*"If you wear a rubber nose for a week,
your life will be changed because you
will get in touch with the joy you can
bring to the world."
-Dr. Hunter "Patch" Adams*

As a young mother I had very little money. We were fortunate to be unfortunate and I would not trade those days for anything. They taught both my children and me many life lessons. It is not how much money you spend on your kids that gives them character or brings them happiness. It is not the number of toys in a toy box that give children courage or teach them creativity. My daughter and son learned these things by sharing and by joining in the fun of creating their own entertainment. This chapter offers suggestions of fun-filled activities and interesting things to do with the children in your life.

"Children's children are a crown to the aged, parents are the pride of their children."
Proverbs 17:6

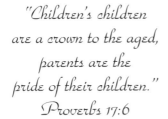

IT'S SHOWTIME!

Fill a large bin or box with assorted odds and ends. Toss in old pots and pans, old clothes, plastic containers, worn out shoes and broken toys. Tell the kids to make up a skit using all the props in the box. This is a great after supper activity. Kids can create a show in the time it takes to finish the supper dishes. Writing and performing skits is very entertaining for everyone. It also helps children to work together to learn how to create something out of nothing. They learn to improvise by making a pasta strainer into a hat or a bed sheet into an evening gown. These backyard shows become terrific memories.

ACTING OUT AT THE TABLE

Create a theme dinner party with the children. We had a Gone With The Wind party once. Each one of us dressed up like a different character in the film. I was Scarlet, of course. I served good old-fashioned southern corn bread and black-eyed peas and we talked in southern accents all evening. We videotaped that evening and we laugh ourselves silly every time we view the video.

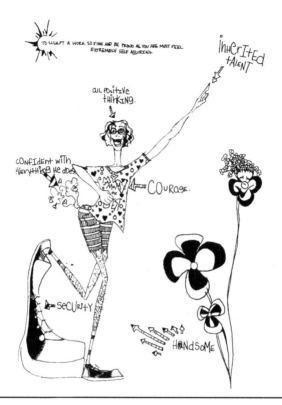

TO SCULPT A WORK SO FINE AND BE PROUD AS YOU ARE MUST FEEL
EXTREMELY SELF ASSURING.

inHerIted tAlent

all positive tHinking.

conFident with everything He does

COURage.

seCURity

HaNdsoMe

THE DO-GOOD AWARD

As a teacher or school official you can start a program in
your school that sends good kids to the principal's office
when they are caught in the act of doing something right.
They get to sign the Do - Good Award Book, get a Do-Good
Certificate and a sticker. The principal may even want to call
the child's parents to let them know they have a great kid in
the family.

At home create an official looking certificate with the
child's name on it and post it on the refrigerator for
everyone to see. A little praise and recognition is a great
motivator when a child is growing up. These awards are
best received when unexpected.

RIDDLE IN THE MIDDLE

Riddles are entertaining at home or in the classroom.
Create a riddle first thing in the morning. It can be given to
the kids at breakfast or slipped into their lunchboxes. The
kids try to solve the riddle throughout the day. Each child
writes his or her name and the answer to the riddle on a
slip of paper and drops it into the answer box at the end of
the school day or at home around the dinner table.
Example: What's black and white and red all over? Answer:
The newspaper! (Read all over.) Choose a time to read over
the answers and see who came up with the correct one.
That person gets to write the riddle for another day.

DALE CARNEGIE FOR KIDS

Speaking in front of an audience is still more frightening then death for most adults. Children are no different. They can be louder than ever and running around the house driving us nuts but ask them to recite the alphabet to company and they turn into shy little introverts. To help kids to learn to speak in front of an audience, have them tell a joke or silly story. Laughter takes the fear out of any situation and speaking in front of an audience is a perfect time to add laughter to the mix.

LUNCHBOX IDEAS

Packing lunches for your family can get pretty boring. However, you can take advantage of the opportunity to say I am thinking of you. Adding simple surprises to someone's lunchbox helps you stay connected to the important people in your life. It may even help them to get through an otherwise difficult day. Here are some fun-filled lunchbox ideas: get some of those candy hearts you find around Valentines day and tape one to the outside of someone's sandwich bag. Add a piece of gum with a note that says, "No matter how hard your work is today if you stick to it you will get it done." Add a nice ripe pear and a note that says, "You and I make a great pair". When you do things like this it makes your loved ones think of you in the middle of the day. It's a fun way to stay connected.

FAMILY PRAISE BOX

At the end of every day each family member writes on a slip of paper one thing they think someone in the family did right that day. At the end of each week or month Mom or Dad empties the box and writes a note to each person listing all the compliments found in the box about them. When a child gets a list of praise from his family it makes him or her want to continue the good work and perhaps even improve upon it. This is also a great way to teach children to be grateful and to show appreciation for the things others do for them.

FUN JOURNAL

Whenever I have a really good time I write about it in my
fun journal. Now I can look back and remember the good
times I have shared with others. This is something you can
do with your children. Keep a fun journal with your kids
this summer. Every night before you tuck them in instead
of reading a story, how about writing one? This is a good
way to keep their writing skills sharp during the summer.
But more important it is something you can do together
that is fun. Who knows, you may be grooming the next
Erma Bombeck or Dave Berry. Go have yourself a fun day
and then write about it.

RIDICULOUS JAR

Take any jar and decorate it to be your ridiculous jar. On slips of paper each family member writes silly, ridiculous things he or she would really like to do. Drop the idea into the family ridiculous jar. Make it a ritual that every Friday night you take turns choosing one idea out of the jar to do as a family. No matter how silly or ridiculous you feel this idea is, it is one you have to follow through with. The sillier or more ridiculous the idea is, the better. One time my son, John, decided it would be a great idea to walk about the backyard with our underpants on our heads! That was the one that made us laugh the most.

TALK TO YOUR CHILDREN

Tonight when the kids say, "There is nothing to do. I'm bored", give them each a piece of paper and ask them to write down the name of someone they really admire. It could be a famous person, a family member or even someone fictitious, like Superwoman. Then ask them to write down what they admire about the person they chose. What makes this person special? Next ask them to list the positive characteristics of their hero. Make a note of the things your child likes about this person that you see in your child. Tell the child about it. Sometimes children do not see the fine qualities they have until someone points them out. You can also try to think up ways that your child can develop some of the qualities they admire in their hero's life. This is a fun way to find out who your children admire. It also starts an interesting conversation between you and your child.

READ 'EM AND LAUGH

This week have each of your children choose something to read out loud that is funny, funny, funny. Some children really do not like to read simply because they are not good readers. One of the best ways to help kids learn to read is to have them read something funny. Suddenly the act of reading is no longer a burden or something to dread. When you add laughter to the mix reading becomes an entertaining and cool thing to do.

BACK YARD ART FESTIVAL

My friend Heidi is a wonderful artist. One summer afternoon she had a backyard art festival. She displayed all of her artwork and invited friends and family to come and take a look. She served wine and cheese and really made a nice afternoon of it. It was great fun and a chance for us all to appreciate her talent and hard work.

Create an art festival of your own by taping large drawings made by your children, to the fence in the backyard. Invite your friends and their children over to take a peek. Serve something to eat and drink and enjoy the artwork.

DINE BY CANDLELIGHT

Tonight set the table a little differently. Put a few candles in the center and turn the lights down low. Surprising things will happen. All of a sudden you will see smiles on your children's faces. They will wonder what you are up to. Remember to notice the flicker of the light on everyone's face. This may be a way to begin a new and different conversation at the dinner table. You can talk about why it is nice to dine by candlelight. Notice the way children all of a sudden have better table manners. It is like a miracle.

PICNIC IN A MINUTE

When you come home from working all day the last thing you want to do is slave over a hot stove. Here is a cool last minute dinner idea. Have an emergency picnic basket ready at all times. Pack it with non-perishable foods like granola bars, raisins and juice boxes. Make sure you have sunscreen, insect repellant, and Band-Aids. For fun add a camera, bubbles, shovels, magnifying glass, and a jump rope. Toss in a few Ziploc bags and wet wipes for easy clean up. Now when the mood strikes you, just pull out the picnic basket and add a few sandwiches and fruit. Presto, you are ready to go. I think last minute fun is the best kind there is.

JERRY SEINFELD QUESTION GAME

Jerry Seinfeld is famous for his thought provoking observational humor. Have a Seinfeld night. Go around the room and ask each family member to think up a Seinfeld sort of question. Think of something you have observed that makes you ponder. Example: Why do we put screws, nuts and bolts in baby food jars? You don't have to answer the question. Some of the questions will make you laugh and some will just get you to think.

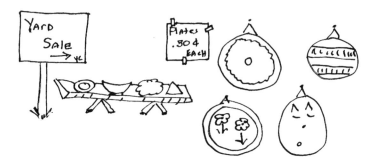

SPECIAL PLATES FOR SPECIAL MOMENTS

Take your children to a flea market or garage sale. Give them each a few dollars to spend but tell them they have to pick out a dish that will be their special dish. It could be a pretty china plate or an antique glass dish. It might be a plastic one with a pretty design or something fun from the fifties. Let the child have whatever dish is in the budget. After you have taken it home and carefully washed it, put it away in a safe place. Whenever the child is sick or just feeling down, use that plate to make him or her feel special. You can also use the plate to mark a special occasion such as a good spelling paper or a wining ball game. No one else will ever use the plate except the child who picked it out. It belongs to only him or her. It's special.

HIDE AND SEEK

Buy several scratch off lottery tickets. Before everyone gets home from work and school, hide them around the house. While you are busy getting dinner ready ask the rest of the family to do several chores. Let them know that while they are folding laundry or putting away toys they just might find a treasure. This keeps everyone amused while you are busy and it gets some of the chores done at the same time.

LAUGHTER CASSEROLE

Tonight instead of telling your children to sit up straight and mind their manners, how about serving them something to laugh about? Give every member of the family something really silly to wear at the dinner table and sit back and listen to the laughter. Silly headbands, red clown noses, goofy glasses or silly hats will make the most serious of family members crack a smile. Nothing brings a family together more than an evening of fun and laughter. Tonight have your self some suppertime fun. Serve up generous helpings of chuckles, giggles, guffaws and snickers.

LIBRARY HISTORY LESSON

A simple trip to the library can be the most fun you have had all week. Looking through old newspapers and magazines can give you a better appreciation for the way you live your life today. It can also be a great source of laughter when you look at some of the hairstyles and clothing from the past. For a good history lesson and a way of understanding how different life was in years past, take a fun trip to the library.

CAMP LIVING ROOM

Take a trip to a comfy campsite where there are no bugs, no rodents and no bears. Set up a tent in your living room. It can be as simple as a few sheets tied to some chairs or as elaborate as setting up a real tent. Now set a fire in the fireplace and actually get some sticks and toast a few marshmallows. Sing some old-fashioned campfire songs and tell some scary stories. This is a great way to put some zing into a ho-hum evening.

POST CARD EXCHANGE

Most children love to get mail. It makes them feel important. But for the most part children find only birthday cards and an occasional holiday card in the mailbox. One way to change that is to start a postcard exchange. Have your children send a postcard with a picture of where you live to your friends and family who live in other parts of the country. Then ask your friends to have their kids send a postcard about their home or town to your kids. Starting a postcard exchange is a fun way for your children to learn about other cities. This is also a great activity for children and their grandparents.

PAPER BAG HAIR TIES

Here is a fun way to do your hair. You do not have to be a
kid to enjoy this but it is a wonderful activity to do with the
kids. It is especially fun at a pajama party. Wet your hair. Rip
strips of brown paper grocery bags and use just like the
expensive ones you buy in the store to wrap around your
hair. Tie to secure and wait until your hair dries to remove
the paper and see the luscious curls. Be sure and take lots
of pictures of all the girls in their paper bag curlers.

POSITIVE 'TIME OUT' KIT

Have your children ever come running in with tears stained faces accusing each other for some wrong doing? Parents can get so frustrated with the noise and commotion that they give everyone a time out. Children may feel they are being treated unfairly, especially if they are not the one who instigated the spat. Make some humorous time out kits for your children. Fill decorative boxes with interesting, fun items to amuse your children while you calmly sort out the situation. The next time sibling rivalry happens stop the unpleasant noise with some fun.

SCHOOL DAY CONVERSATION

When the kids come home from school this afternoon have a conversation with them. Do not ask, "How was school today?" because you can be sure the answer will be, "OK." And for goodness sake do not say, "What did you learn in school today?", because we know the answer will most definitely be, "Nothing." Try a different question tonight. Ask the kids, "What is the funniest thing that happened in school today?" Or, "Who's the funniest kid or teacher in school?" Children will always talk about something they think is funny. Now you have a conversation going. You are communicating with your kids and that is a good thing. (This works with the adults in your life too.) Have yourself a fun conversation with your kids today.

During a long trip even kids can get bored. The next six pages offer a variety of games to play while riding in the car.

CHILDREN'S TRAVEL JOURNAL

When traveling for more than a day or two children can get very tired. Give them something to keep them interested in the trip. Have each child create a scrapbook filled with his or her memories of the trip. Before the trip create an idea box for each child to use when making the travel journal. Give each child a map before the trip. Ask them to cut out the states they will be traveling through on the trip. Add the clipped states to the idea box along with colored paper, glue sticks, tape, pictures from magazines of cars, trucks, hotels, beds, crayons or colored pencils, and stickers. While on the trip they can use anything in their idea box to make their travel journal. Children can collect things during the trip such as souvenirs, a brochure from a hotel or restaurant, children's menus, postcards or brochures from places you visit such as museums or theme parks. It may even be a good idea to give each child his own disposable camera. This is not only a great way to keep kids interested and happy during the trip, it also is a wonderful remembrance for years to come.

JR. PHOTOJOURNALIST

Suggest that the older children in your family become photojournalists while on a trip. Allow them to use a Polaroid camera, video camera or digital camera and computer to create a high tech essay documenting the trip. This is a great way to teach your child about the job of a journalist. He must document the day's events on film, review the shots, edit out the bad ones and write essays about the day's events. The results can be used as a great present for grandparents or a project for school. Either way it is the best way I have found to keep a young person happy on the road.

ABC CAR GAME

Here is a game we used to play that helped pass the time and often made us laugh. Choose a category such as history, famous people, foods or animals. The first player says one item from the category: pizza, for example. The next player must come up with an item in the same category that begins with the last letter of that word, as in the example below. Each player has a turn at coming up with a word. The game continues until someone is stumped. Once you are stumped you are out of the game. The last player to come up with the proper word wins. Example: pizza-apple-endive-egg-grilled cheese and so on.

I SPY

The first player chooses an object inside the car that everyone else can see and says, "I spy with my little eye, something that starts with..." and gives the letter that it starts with, such as "T" for tape deck.

Everyone else in the car shouts out the names of objects they can see that start with that letter. Teeth? Turn signal? Tee shirt? The first one who guesses the correct word is the next to choose an object and say 'I spy...

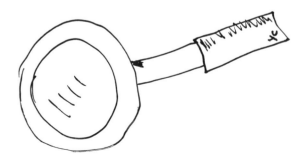

CAR TÊTE-À-TÊTE

When my children were very small we lived in Tennessee and most of our extended family lived in New York. That was one long car ride for two small children. I found it was a good time to actually talk to the kids. I would tell them a story about something that happened to me when I was a child. It always amazed me at how interested they were to learn about my childhood. I believe it brought us closer together. You can also ask your children to tell a story about something they don't think you know about. You will be amazed at what you may learn about each other.

SLUG BUG

During a car ride everyone looks for Volkswagens. When a Volkswagen Beetle is spotted the player says, 'Slug Bug!' and gets one point. If a VW Van or Bus is spotted shout out, "Bug Bus!" For this the player gets two points! The player who gets to 25 points first wins the game.

LICENSE PLATE BINGO

Before the trip create Bingo cards with five rows and five columns. In the middle square, write FREE. Fill the other 24 squares randomly with two letters or two-digit numbers (for example, NY, 12, PA, 87 W4). Each player gets one card and a marker pen. Players watch the letters and numbers on license plates of the cars and trucks as they pass. For example, if the license plate in front of you is FWC168, it will match any square on your card that says: FW, WC C1 16 or 68. As soon as you see the two-letter or number/letter combination on a license plate matching one on your Bingo card, cross out that square. The first person to cross out five squares in a row—horizontally, vertically, or diagonally—says 'Bingo!' and wins the game.

ROAD SIGN BINGO

Before your trip make up some Bingo cards with common road sign words, such as: SLOW, STOP, YIELD, SNOW, SLIPPERY, TUNNEL, CURVE, CHILDREN, HOSPITAL, TOLL, FOOD, etc. Players use words from signs they see to mark the cards. The word on the sign must match the word on the card exactly. As soon as you see a word matching one on your Bingo card, cross out that square. The first person to cross out five squares in a row—horizontally, vertically, or diagonally—says 'Bingo!' and wins the game.

B	I	N	G	O
FW	14	49	12	LA
32	NY	40	60	51
WC	01	FrEE	PA	49
LP	76	NY	CR	TN
42	YS	NJ	69	91

B	I	N	G	O
STOP	SNOW	Lodging	go	Slow
Drive Thru	Yield	go	Curve	STOP
Food	Toll	FrEE	Tunnel	go
Police	Food	go	Toll	stop
Yield	STOP	Curve	Turn	off

Motivation and Creativity

Techniques to Inspire

"It is well known that humor, more than anything else in the human makeup, can afford an aloofness and an ability to rise above any situation, even if only for a few seconds."
- Victor Frankl

Whether you are a stay at home parent, a middle manager or a Fortune 500 executive you know how easy it is to get stuck in a boring, routine life and only fantasize about what could have been. In this chapter you will find techniques for breaking through the negative barriers that stop you from reaching your goals. Quick and easy exercises help you let go of pessimistic thoughts and create positive productive thought patterns. Try doing one exercise a week or creating some of your own. We all need an action plan for living the joyful life we deserve both at work and at home. This chapter will move you from your comfort zone into the true you zone. If you always do what you've always done then you will always get what you've always had. Start here, add some fun and end up wherever you want to be with these simple ways to motivate yourself to be the best that you can be.

"He that is of a
merry heart has
a continual feast."
- Proverbs 15:15

FOCUS ON SOMETHING GOOD

If I laid a two by four stud on the floor and tried to walk across it, I could do it without any problem. But if I laid that same two by four stud ten stories high, between two buildings and tried to walk across it I do not think I could make it. In fact I do not think I would attempt it at all because all I would be focusing on is falling. It is important to focus on what we want to accomplish rather than on what we are afraid might happen. Think about what you want to create in your life. Focus on achieving it. Focus on successfully accomplishing your goal.

21-DAY CHALLENGE

If you have a habit that you really want to change take
the twenty-one day challenge. Experts say if you do anything
for twenty-one days in a row you will create a new habit.
This is how I stopped using cream and sugar in my coffee. I
drank it black for twenty-one days. Now I like it that way. At
first I didn't like the taste without the sweetness of the
cream and sugar but after twenty-one days of drinking it
black I no longer wanted to add anything that would take
away from the flavor of good, strong coffee. Start or change
a habit today. In twenty-one days it will be part of you.

INTERNAL DIALOGUE

Do you look in the mirror and disgustingly say to yourself, "Fat thighs! Pot belly! Help!"? This is negative talk. Replacing it with some positive internal dialogue will actually help you live healthier. Each time you make a negative remark to yourself stop and replace it with something positive. Look in the mirror and say, "Strong thighs, soft belly, I'm doing great." Positive inner talk will eventually motivate you to emulate those thoughts.

COPY YOUR HERO

Do you want to be a talented singer, an impressive athlete or a skillful cook? Are you striving to be a business owner or to move up a step on the corporate ladder? Would you like to write a book or be a better parent? The best way to accomplish any goal is to find someone who is already successful and model him or her. What habits do they have? Where do they hang out? What do they eat? Who do they spend time with? What do they wear? Act like you already are what you want to be. If you want to be an impressive athlete, copy what your idol does. Does he get up at the crack of dawn to exercise? Does he eat certain foods? Does he get a certain amount of sleep? Does he smoke or drink alcohol? If you live your life they way your role model does you will soon find yourself closer to your goal. The truth is that our heroes are just the same as we are. The only difference is that they have achieved more. We can be every bit as successful and fulfilled as our hero is. By studying the people we admire the most we learn to follow the paths they take. We can grow into that which we admire – so choose someone to emulate. Fill your life with this person. Put his or her pictures all around you. Read about your hero. Memorize his quotes. Observe his work. Become an expert on this person's life. You can succeed when you copy someone who is already successful.

TAKE A VACATION FROM YOUR COMFORT ZONE

Do something today that is not in your comfort zone – just to see if you can. What does it feel like to be that daring? Ask someone that you don't know that well, to go to lunch with you. Go on a roller coaster ride. Go to a pet store and pet a dog or pick up a snake. Anything that you normally would not think of doing is what you should be doing today. WOW! Stretch that comfort zone!

PLANT YOUR LIFE GARDEN

Are you wondering where all the flowers have gone? Ask yourself what have you been planting? Are you planting weeds or did you put a beautiful red tulip bulb into the ground? What kind of nourishment are you giving it? The truth is that we reap what we sow. Plant yourself some positive seeds, nourish them with solid, positive reinforcement and watch your garden grow.

START A FUN SAVINGS HABIT

Can you save money? Start small. Find a funky sort of piggy bank. Add your change every day, at the same time, into the bank. Do not spend it on anything, no matter what. By doing this you are giving yourself the proof you need that you do have the ability to save money. You can follow through and accomplish something long term. When your bank is filled count the change and use the money to buy something you really want. You'll be surprised at how quickly all that change adds up and you will be proud of yourself for learning how easy saving can be.

MY FANTASY REALITY

If it is hard for you to imagine your potential, you might want to begin by expressing it as a fantasy. Write a story about who you would like to be. Close your eyes for a moment and dream. What would you be doing if there were absolutely no way that you could fail? Take a moment and describe your day as if everything were just the way you dreamed. Start with the moment you get up in the morning. Where do you live? Whom do you live with? How much money do you make? What do you look like? How do you dress? What are you most proud of? Because your subconscious mind does not know you are fantasizing you will begin to create the necessary blueprint for your action plan. You cannot reach your ideal self without a picture of what that self is. Once you have written your fantasy, read it aloud. Do this every night before you fall asleep. It will not be long before your action plan becomes your life plan.

TELL YOURSELF A BIG LIE

Make up a big lie about how successful you are! Think big and be creative. Anything that you would like to have, be or do can come true. If you dare to believe this you can also direct your brain to think that it has already happened! Write the lie down on paper. It is the truth about who you can be. When you can see it, hear it and feel it then it will become reality.

BECOME A CHILD

As adults we seem to be always looking for ways to become more inspired, more creative and more energized. Here is a simple way to do just that. Spend an entire day with a child. Do whatever the child wants to do. Try to see the world through the child's eyes. Make no judgments about what it is you spend your time doing, just follow the child's lead. Become a child for the entire day. Enjoy childlike enthusiasm. Pretend right along with the child. Woody Allen once said, "To find real humor, sit at the children's table." Become a child for just one day and watch what happens. Your entire perspective on the world may change.

WRITE WITH THE WRONG HAND

How can you learn a new task or change an old one? If you are right handed try writing with your left hand and if you are left handed try using your right hand. This is difficult and may seem almost impossible. However, if I were to offer you a million dollars if you could learn to write equally well with either hand do you think you could accomplish that? Would you be motivated to practice night and day for a million dollars? The problem is not that you can't write equally well with both hands it is that you have not learned how to do it. The truth is we can learn to do anything better with practice. The same principle is true for reprogramming the way we think. Motivate yourself to think positive thoughts for five minutes each morning. Soon you will have reprogrammed your mind by practicing to think positive. The desire to change is the motivation you need.

START A WAY OUT JOURNAL

A Way Out Journal is full of ideas that can help you find your way out of bad situations. Write down the situations in your life that you would like to change. Think about this scenario: I'm looking around my kitchen like a rat looking for cheese. I open every cupboard. I stand and look at the contents of my refrigerator like a soldier looking for the enemy and I cannot find anything good to eat. I see the whipped topping in the freezer, the peanut butter in the cupboard and the chocolate chips on the shelf. I think about them all mixed together in a fat and sugar filled treat. I am going to ruin my diet. What I need is a way out. Open your journal. Look at your list: call a friend who talks for hours, get out of the house, log on to the computer, run an errand, paint my nails. Choose an item from your list and do it. You will have found a way out.

USE PROPS TO STIMULATE CREATIVITY

Nothing stifles creativity more than boredom! To wake up your creative mind bring in some props. If you want to think like a winner, wear a gold medal. Put a sign on your wastebasket that says, 'IN BOX'. When someone asks for your help wave a magic wand, smile and say, "No problem, I'll get right to it."

Psychologists tell us that bright colors help us to think outside the box and come up with interesting ideas. Maybe a purple boa will get those creative juices flowing. Go all out and put on a multi colored clown wig. Wear it all day long! Have yourself a fun filled creative day.

INTERROGATE YOURSELF

Have you ever heard the expression, "I'm lower then a snake in a rut."? Now that is low! When you are down that low it is hard to dig your way up and out. Have you ever wondered why you just cannot seem to get moving up and out? You want to accomplish something but you just cannot seem to get going. Sit your self down under a bright light and interrogate yourself. What is it that isn't working for you right now? What do you think you need to change? Ask yourself what is it that you really want to happen? What is your first step? What needs to happen in order to know that your plan is working? What is your goal? Once you have the answers to these questions you are well on your way out of the rut.

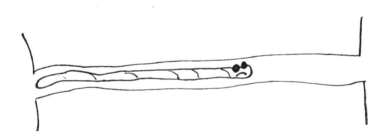

$100. INVESTMENT

Have you ever listened to the flight attendant on a plane tell you to put the mask on yourself first and then take care of your children? It is important to take good care of yourself all the time, not just on the plane. Take one hundred dollars and invest in YOU. Take a class. Hire a maid for the day. Join a gym. Hire a trainer. Buy a set of tapes or books on a subject dear to your heart. When you do something just for you, you are telling yourself that you are of value. Sometimes we are so busy taking care of others we forget about the most important person of all. If you do not take care of yourself first, you wont be able to take care of anyone else.

WHAT YOU SEE IS WHAT YOU GET

Make a conscious visual effort to reach your mind. On brightly colored paper, write out fifty positive statements or quotes that relate in some way to your goal. Cut them out and paste, tack or tape them everywhere. Put them in drawers, on the mirror, in the medicine cabinet, on your dresser, under your hat, on your car, on the dashboard, on the visor and in the kitchen. Deliberately feed your spirit with optimistic ideas that you want to live by.

Example: Every day in every way I'm getting better and better. I am STRONG. I am HAPPY. How I act is who I will become. What the mind can conceive and believe it can achieve. My mind creates my future.

AFFIRMING MY FUTURE

"I will act now! I will act now! I will act now!" Repeat these words each day until the words become as much a part of you as your breathing is a part of you. With these words we can condition our minds to meet every challenge.

Write out twenty positive affirmations associated with your goal. They must be written in the present tense, as if you have already succeeded. For example: I am healthy vs. I will be or I am going to be healthy. The most powerful affirmations begin with "I am". Repeat your affirmations aloud twice a day, morning and night. Believe that you will accomplish your goals.

EXERCISE EVERY DAY

We all know that exercise is good for us but some of us just cannot seem to find the time or do not like to exercise. Fancy health clubs can be a bit intimidating or out of our price range. Make exercise fun. Start a fitness club with your friends, family, neighbors or co-workers. Take a poll and find out what kind of physical activities they actually like to do. Plan a fifteen-minute a day walking club or going swing dancing every Friday night. Dance in each other's living rooms. A little bit of exercise every single day, can make a big difference in how you feel. It can change your mood and give you added energy. Best of all it can be fun.

BE ALL YOU CAN BE

When people come to our country for the first time, many are absolutely amazed at what they see. They are impressed with tall buildings, beautiful landscapes and friendly people. Almost everyone who visits here sees something that many of us take for granted: opportunity. In this country you really can be anything you want to be. Many people use excuses, like bad health, lack of education or age to explain why they could not succeed. Remember President Franklin Roosevelt led our country from a wheel chair. President Harry Truman never went to college and many people thought that John Kennedy was much too young to ever become president. These were great excuses...that were never used. Give up your excuses today. The next time you start to use an excuse...stop...it could very well be the start of an opportunity.

TURN UP THE VOLUME

Are you sluggish at your desk? Put on a favorite CD and turn up the volume. Nothing motivates more quickly than good, loud music. Try dancing around the office a little bit. Good dance music or spiritual tunes can wake you up and get you going. Music is an amazing mood lifter.

100 INSTANT IDEAS

Is there a problem that you need to solve? Write the problem at the top of a sheet of paper. Each morning before you begin to work take out that sheet of paper and write down twenty ideas that can solve the problem. These ideas do not all have to be amazing, incredible, mind blowing ideas. In fact some of them may be silly or downright ridiculous. Do this every day for five days and you will have a sheet of paper with one hundred ideas. From these one hundred ideas you will find the one that works for you. By forcing yourself to generate twenty ideas a day you are putting yourself in position to think more creatively. This process will lead you to the one idea that will solve the problem.

DREAM BIG

You can be the builder of your dreams. Go through old magazines and cut out pictures and words that represent the person you want to be, the way you want to look, a place you want to go or something you want to have. Try to use color pictures. Once you have arranged the pictures and words that represent all your desires, start gluing them to a poster board and call it your Dream Board. Put your dream board in a place where you will see it every day. A visual display of what you want in life sends subconscious messages to your brain. These messages eventually become actions that can make your dream board a reality. Your entire family can build a dream board. This is a great way to find out what the other people in your family dream about. And it's FUN!

MAKE A LIST

Today, make a list of the people in your life who really believe in you and help you stay positive and upbeat. Who encourages you? Who makes you feel invincible? Keep your list in front of you while you work. Make sure you spend time with someone from your list of positive, encouraging people each day. We are a product of what goes into our minds every day. We need to spend time each day with people who can fill our minds with positive, happy and encouraging thoughts.

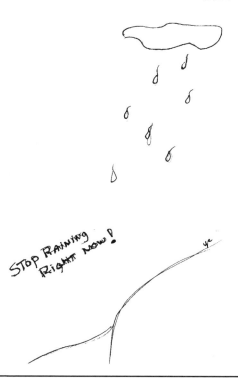

STOP RAINING RIGHT NOW!

MIND CONTROL

Don't waste your time complaining or worrying about things you have no control over. Are you in charge of the rain and the sunshine? Is it your job to secure a solid economy for our country? Are you really able to control what other people think? If your answer is no to any of these questions then don't waste your time or energy thinking about, complaining about or worrying about the things you cannot change. Try to concentrate on what you CAN control. Who is in charge of your actions? Who handles your thoughts? Who chooses what you read and what television shows you watch? You are in control over whom you hug and how much you laugh. If you concern yourself with the things you can control your life will become easier.

Celebration, Tradition and Family

Hoilday and Celebration Ideas

"In order to get the full value
of Joy you must have someone
to divide it with."
- Mark Twain

Love and support from family certainly adds to a joyful life. Family is not always made up of blood relatives. Family is anyone you truly love and would do anything for. People who make you smile when times are hard and who will always be there for you - they are family. Whatever the make up of your family, holidays and family celebrations can be major productions. We have pumpkins to carve, cards to write, gifts to buy, wrap and send. There are eggs to decorate and baskets to fill. There are trees to buy, candles to light, cookies to bake, parties to plan, turkeys to roast, and for gosh sakes somebody please clean the bathroom! We want the best for our families and in the process we get kids bouncing off walls from sugar overdose, mothers scrounging for Prozac and fathers wondering how it all happened. If you are feeling that your celebrations do not measure up to your expectations you may be doing too much. In this chapter you will fine simple ideas that will bring smiles, laughter and true joy to any celebration. These simple suggestions show you how to appreciate the good times and put spirit and laughter into any celebration.

"Sing to him a new song,
play skillfully,
and shout for joy."
- Psalm 33:3

A Big Hand for Topo Gigio!

FAMILY NIGHT

When I was a little girl I looked forward to Sunday night when we would all gather around the black and white TV set and watch the Ed Sullivan show. Sunday night was always our night to be together as a family. I can almost smell the popcorn. That was a tradition we could count on. You can start a tradition with your family. Ask each family member what their favorite funny movie is and then go out and rent them all and surprise your family with a comedy night! Pop a big bowl of hot buttered popcorn, cuddle up on the couch with the family and laugh together. Spending an evening with the most important people in your life is a great way to stay connected.

SPECIAL NAME TABLE CLOTH

Make a family heirloom by taking a simple tablecloth and having everyone sign it on special occasions. After everyone has gone home embroider over the written name to make the signature last forever. If you are not crafty you can use this same idea the way my cousins did. Each time they had a birthday party they asked the birthday girl or boy to sign and date their tablecloth with a special pen to mark the event. When they used the signature tablecloth it was always covered with clear plastic to protect the signatures. We had great fun reading over the names and remembering the day each one was written.

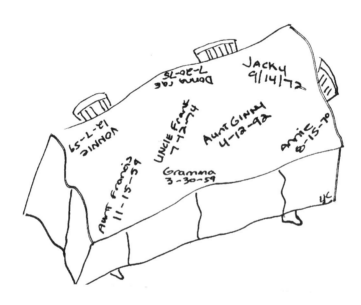

CONVERSATION AND LAUGHTER FOREVER TAPE

Many years ago my father and I made a trip to visit my great uncle and aunt. Dad was nearly 85 and my uncle was close to 100 years old. I took a small tape recorder with me and recorded our conversations that day. This simple tape has brought me so much joy. Whenever I want to hear my father's laughter or my uncle's thick Italian accent, I turn on my tape recorder. I sit with a cup of coffee and close my eyes and they are with me once again. Record the conversations and laughter of your parents, aunts and uncles, grandparents and siblings. Some of our fondest memories are the times our family makes us laugh.

JANUARY 1ST: NEW YEAR CHOICES

It is the beginning of a New Year and time to make the dreaded New Year Resolution. We think that this is the time to set new goals and make changes in our lives. Somehow we believe that magically this year we will keep those resolutions. A few days or weeks go by and we are discouraged because we did not follow through. This year just decide to consistently make better choices. It is easy to keep this promise. I choose to keep laughter and humor in my life every day. I choose to be grateful every day for all that I have. I choose to eat healthier foods. I choose to read more books and watch less television. Somehow making these statements makes it easier to follow through because each time you are faced with temptation you are in control you make the choice.

THE TASTE OF HOME

Are there any particular foods that come to mind when you think of home? I always think of sauce on Sunday with oversized meatballs and mountains of pasta. My children think of cornbread and pinto beans, broccoli and corn casserole and fried chicken. What is the tradition of your family? What aromas come to mind when you think of your mother's kitchen? All I have to do is smell green peppers cooking and my grandmother comes to mind instantly. Ask your family what their favorite dishes are and make them often. Too many times we depend on fast food and microwave ovens to give us quick, easy meals. It is okay to use these shortcuts from time to time but just be sure your children do not end up thinking about you every time they hear a the microwave buzz.

REAL POPCORN IS THE SECRET

We are a microwave society. We get the instant
gratification but what we are missing are the aromas and
the down home flavor that comes from making things from
scratch. I refuse to microwave popcorn. Mine is made on
top of the stove in my popcorn pan - an old stainless steel
pot with a dome lid. The popcorn is perfect every time.
There is nothing better than the smell of home popped
corn all over the house. A big pan of warm, home popped
corn is a simple pleasure and a memorable tradition.

JANUARY 8TH: BIRTHDAY OF "THE KING"

Celebrate the King of Rock and Roll's birthday by having a rockin' party. Invite friends over and play only Elvis music. The guys can slick their hair back and the gals can wear pony-tails. Schedule dance contests or Elvis impersonator contests. Serve peanut butter and banana sandwiches. Raise your upper lip and say, "Thank you, thank you very much."

JANUARY 15TH: MARTIN LUTHER KING DAY

This is a great day to celebrate equality and love for all mankind. Set aside time to discus civil rights and how it has changed our country. Use this day to help your children to understand the important message of Dr. King. Read aloud his famous, "I have a dream." Speech.

WINTER BEACH PARTY

When the snow and ice pile up we can get discouraged.
We can ease out of the winter blues by doing something fun
and exhilarating. This is the perfect time for a beach party.
Fill a kiddy pool with water and add a few floating beach
balls. Or fill it with sand, pails and shovels. Invite your
guests to wear summer clothes and straw hats and be sure
to serve foods like corn on the cob, salt potatoes, barbecued
chicken, watermelon and gallons of ice cream. It's a great
way to beat the winter blues for just one afternoon. Turn on
a sun lamp, pull out those old beach boy songs and treat
yourself to a hot summer day!

CELEBRATE LIFE

The next time something rather uneventful happens in your family or at the office make a big deal out of it. Celebrate it as if it is something absolutely tremendous. When your child brings home a good grade on a paper take the whole family out to dinner to celebrate. When someone in your office wins a new account celebrate as if it were the biggest account your firm has ever had. There is no law that says you celebrate only the really big events in life. Make every day spectacular.

FEBRUARY 14ᵀᴴ: TRADE LOVE LETTERS

This is a great way to celebrate Valentines Day. Trade
letters with the love of your life. Write about things you truly
love about one another. Include the traits that you admire
and add a sentence or two about why you respect each
other. Then over a glass of fine wine, read the letters out
loud to one another.

MAY: MOTHERS DAY SURPRISE

How often do we think about something our mom did for us or said to us? We always intend to let her know we are thinking of her, but our lives get busy and we never make the call. If this sounds familiar start writing love notes whenever you have a fond memory of mom. Collect these love notes in a pretty box. Give it to mom with a note that says, "Whenever you think of me take out one of these notes to read and know that I am thinking of you." This is a marvelous way to connect with the most important person in your life.

POETRY IN MOTION

There is nothing more soothing than having someone read to you. When the one you love is doing the reading it is very special. We read to children before they go to sleep, however not many of us read to each other. Find a poem or reading that has meaning for you and take turns reading out loud to each other before bed.

MAY: MEMORIAL DAY

For many families Memorial Day means get the grill and lawn chairs out of their winter hideaways and plan a family picnic. But this is really a day for remembering those that have lost their lives protecting our country. What a great time to ask the older members of your family to tell how they celebrated this important day. My mom remembers a very special tradition. Her family (and most everyone else in the small town where she lived) walked from the church to the cemetery carrying flowers to honor the veterans who lost their lives in service to our country. She said it really was a moving experience for her as a small child to see all the flags marking the graves of those who made the ultimate sacrifice. These memories add interesting stories to family histories. So light up the grill and get the horseshoes out of the garage and ask your family to tell you a story about their celebrations. You may be surprised at what you learn.

JUNE: BASTILLE DAY

Bastille Day is a national holiday in France. It is the celebration of the storming of the Bastille (a French prison) and the beginning of the French revolution. It is a very big day in France. Why not celebrate by doing everything French today? Start your day with French toast, order French fries for lunch or go to a fancy French restaurant. Just for fun, speak in a French accent. Every day can be fun and new. All you need is a good excuse to do something a little bit different.

JUNE 14TH: FLAG DAY

What a great day to read a story to the children about Betsy Ross or developing a game with questions about the flag. You can give flag related gifts as prizes. Utilize this day to learn about the history of our flag and in the process share an entertaining learning experience with the children in your life.

George

ABE

JULY 4TH: INDEPENDENCE DAY

On July 4th we celebrate our country's birthday with fireworks and backyard parties or picnics. My sister has always had the best July 4th celebrations. Everyone must arrive in costume. Since it is really a birthday party we all get presents but we have to work for them. We are each given the name of a person in history and we have to act like them until the rest of the family can guess who we are. When we succeed at these Forth of July charades we have earned a red, white or blue present.

OCTOBER 31ST: HALLOWEEN

Halloween does not have to be an expensive holiday. I loved rummaging through my parents' clothes looking for something to wear. One year I wore an old hat with one of dad's suits and put charcoal all over my face. I'm not sure what I was supposed to be. Let the kids go searching in the closets and use their imaginations to put together a great Halloween outfit. Anything that sparkles will sure to delight your little girl and an eyebrow pencil can make the nicest little boy into a scary old troll! Open up the closets and pull out all that glitters and see what fun you can create.

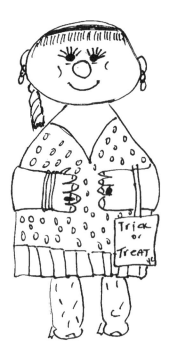

DECEMBER: CHANUKAH

No matter what your religious background, it is a good idea to research the meaning behind other people's holidays. When I read about Chanukah, I was impressed with the determination and faith of the Jewish people. Chanukah or The Feast of Lights commemorates the Jewish people's victory in the first recorded battle for religious freedom. It was a battle for the right to worship God in their own traditional way. A miracle occurred when the eternal light of the temple which had been put out by the Syrians was rekindled and remained burning for eight days even though the oil available was sufficient for only one day. When you look at the bright lights and feel the warmth of the Chanukah candles let it be a reminder of the warmth and strength of the Jewish family. And of what a joy it is for all of us to have religious freedom. Happy Chanukah.

NOVEMBER – DECEMBER:
THANKSGIVING TO CHRISTMAS CHAIN

Do you have children in your family who are always asking, "How many more days till Christmas, Mommy?" Here is a remedy for that constant holiday question. At Thanksgiving after the dishes are done and most everyone except the children are passed out on the couch. Get out the construction paper and collect the children. Make a holiday chain - one link for every day until Christmas Eve. Then each night before the children go to bed they take off one link. This way they can easily count how many days are left till the big event.

FAMILY HOLIDAY COOKBOOK

The holidays are a time to get out your favorite recipes and share the flavors with loved ones. Ask everyone to bring a delightful, taste-tempting dish to the holiday table. Also ask for copies of the recipe for every member of the family. Collect the copies as your guests arrive and put them nicely in a folder or binder along with a few holiday snapshots or maybe a written note about the day. Before each guest leaves hand them your holiday surprise - everyone goes home with the family recipes and a few fun snapshots to start a family holiday cookbook.

DECEMBER: CHORE LIST

Make a list of twenty-four things you need to do before Christmas that your children could help you with. Write the numbers one to twenty-five in red and green marker on twenty-five envelopes. Slip a note inside each envelope with one of your list items – this can be anything you need to do from polish the silver to buy a present for your teacher to put up the Christmas tree, to read a Christmas story. String the envelopes on a ribbon or tape them to a wall so they can be opened daily in order. You will have organized your holiday but more importantly you will have spent time with your children in preparation for an important family tradition.

SPECIAL DAY

If you have a child in your life make time for a special day. One year instead of giving my nieces and nephews gifts for their birthdays I decided to spend a day with each of them doing whatever they wanted to do. My niece is a wonderful dancer and has been taking lessons nearly all her life. She and I went out to a fancy restaurant and then to see a live performance of "The Nutcracker" in a beautiful theatre. My nephew wanted to spend the night at my house, play cards for money and then go to a racetrack where we could actually get in the cars and race. We had a great time with his choices. Another day my younger nieces and I enjoyed a day of fun at a children's museum followed by an adventure at an Asian restaurant. Giggles were loud and constant around the table as we ate foods we'd never heard of and used a sauce that was so hot we nearly exploded. The girls spent the night at my house where we all dressed up in old clothes hats and long strings of pearls. Laughter was a major part of this gathering. Gifts come and go but memories like this last forever.

PROGRESSIVE DINNER

When I was first married our neighborhood had Progressive Dinner Parties all the time. A group of friends got together and started at one house for drinks and hors dourves. They moved on to the next house for the salad and soup that was followed with the main course at a third house and finished with dessert and drinks at the last house. The great part of this event is that no one person has the burden of creating the entire evening. Everyone enjoys being the guest.

NOVEMBER: THANKSGIVING PRESENTS

My friend Laura shared this wonderful tradition with me. You know we all complain that everyone is rushing the seasons. Here is an idea that will stretch the holiday season a bit. As you get together to celebrate Thanksgiving give everyone a small gift—one with a Christmas theme. It can be a Santa pin, or jingle bell earrings...or for the guys how bout some Holly Socks? If you give those gifts at Christmastime there is no time to use them until the next year. Using this idea they will be used for a full month before Christmas.

Making a Christmas present a Thanksgiving holiday tradition will bring smiles to everyone's face.

NOVEMBER: THANKSGIVING PRAYER

Families all across America gather together to celebrate Thanksgiving with pumpkin pie and way too much turkey and stuffing. As you are sitting around the table have each person mention what they are most grateful for. A variation on this idea can be to turn to the person on your right and tell him or her why you are grateful for having them in your life. Cherish and be thankful for the most precious gifts, the people in your life. Have a wonderful thankful Thanksgiving!

DECEMBER: HOLIDAY COOKIE PARTY

Do you have friends with whom you really like to spend time and with whom you would love to celebrate the holidays but all of a sudden it is January and you never really connected? Here is a way for you to spend an entire afternoon laughing with them and still get all your holiday baking completed. Invite your closest friends to your home and ask them to bring their favorite holiday cookie recipe and ingredients for a yuletide bakeoff. After rolling and mixing and tasting each other's cookie dough share good talk and holiday cheer while the aromas from a kitchen full of cookies fill the air. When all the cookies are baked everyone takes a variety home. This is a wonderful way to stay connected with friends and still get some of the chores out of the way... and so much fun.

HOLIDAY FUN CLOWN NOSE STYLE

When you are busy making lists of all the things that have to be done for the holiday festivities do not forget to put some unexpected fun on that list. Consider making it mandatory that everyone wear a bright red clown nose for the entire evening. You cannot help but laugh when you see your relatives in a clown nose. To ensure an abundance of laughter wear the noses through all the festivities including dinner. Give your family something to remember this holiday season. Add a little unexpected silliness to your celebration and then laugh and laugh. Be sure and take lots of pictures.

DECEMBER: CHRISTMAS BIRTHDAY CAKE

Christians all over the world celebrate Christmas with gifts and cards and wonderful things from the kitchen. With all the hustle and bustle going on we sometimes lose sight of the real meaning behind all this fun. Christians are celebrating the birth of Jesus Christ. So it is really a birthday party! Next Christmas Eve bake a birthday cake. It is a wonderful way to remind us of the real reason for the season. Merry Christmas!

GIFTS FROM THE ANCESTORS

Do you have a family tradition that has been handed down from generation to generation? Can you answer the child's question, "Why do we do that?" Do the children know that you do certain things because they are traditions? Our Christmas Eve tradition was to have twelve different kinds of fish served at midnight. The fish represented Christ's twelve disciples. Our house always smelled like a fish market that day. Every counter had bowls of fresh fish staring up at us. It was very important to my father to have this meal. He was carrying down a tradition that was given to him from his father and his father before him. There is something about this that gives us strength. To know that those who have lived before us are able to touch our lives in this way is very comforting.

DECEMBER: CHRISTMAS EVE GIFT GIVING

Everyone anticipates traditional gift giving. Why not begin the laughter and fun early? After Christmas Eve dinner serve a bag of gag gifts for dessert. Items like monster feet slippers, a jingle bell bra or a checkbook that cries are sure to bring the celebrations to a happy, laugh filled conclusion.

DECEMBER: NEW YEARS EVE

Instead of making the same old resolutions that we seldom ever keep, make a list of all the things you accomplished during the year. Once you start writing you will be surprised at how long a list you have. Somehow looking at your successes puts you in a better place to begin the New Year. Then you are ready to go out and have a great New Year. Remember to add a little silliness now and then.

TRADITION

When I was a little girl we ate Sunday dinner in the dining room. We used the good china and silver and a linen tablecloth and we had our Sunday dinner together as a family. I could count on that every Sunday. After dinner we stayed around the table and laughed and talked for hours. It was a special tradition that brought us together as a family. With every one so busy today it is important to find time to connect. Start a tradition with your family. Share a special meal. Bring your family together around the table and remember to serve the laughter.

*"Life is not measured
by the breaths we take
but by the moments
that take our breath away."*

INVITATION AND FREE GIFT

What does your family do to celebrate holidays and how do you bring joy and laughter to your workplace? If you have used humor and laughter to get through a difficult situation or if you have added silliness to your work environment Yvonne is interested to learn more about it. We cannot answer every letter or email. Send us your address. Any contributor of a story or silly idea we use in a future publication will get a free gift in the mail. Please send to:

Vice President in Charge of Ideas
Crack-A-Smile Seminars
PMB #231
4736 Onondaga Blvd.
Syracuse, NY 13219
1-888-BE-SILLY
Yvonne@crack-a-smile.com

For information about having Yvonne
as Key Note Speaker at your next conference or meeting
email her at *Yvonne@crack-a-smile.com*
or call 1-888-BE-SILLY.

OTHER BOOKS BY YVONNE CONTE

Serious Laughter provides a wealth of ideas and practical suggestions of how to add humor and laughter to your life. This book provides easy to understand information in an entertainingly friendly, but very authoritative way. In addition, it is filled with action packed drawings that create excitement for the reader.

Serious Laughter teaches the medical and spiritual benefits of humor and shows you how to find the laughter. This book gives example after example of how to go about adding these aspects to your life both at work and at home. But more than that Serious Laughter takes you by the hand and shows you how to deal with stress and worry, anger, resentfulness, fear, doubt, insecurity, jealousy, rage and depression. It is an excellent source of motivational material that will keep you thinking positive. Partly autobiographical this book proves to be a delight to read, as each page is very conversational and personal.

This fun-filled book is a gradual awakening to the joys of laughter and an introduction to a wonderful vehicle that will help us through the difficult times and simply make the good times more meaningful.

Price: $16.95, plus shipping & handling

Frankie Wonders...What Happened Today? This book is a look through a 4 year olds eyes at the horrific events of September 11th. Little Frankie knows something is wrong but he doesn't know what and he doesn't know why his family is so sad.

The story guides Frankie through feelings of anger, confusion and fear. It is a book not only for children but for adults as well. Everyone needs what Frankie needs.

All net profits from the publication of this book will be donated to The Children's Aid Society in New York City to help them to continue to counsel the children who may be depressed or anxious.

Price: $12.00, plus shipping & handling

TOY STORE

GROUCHO MARX NOSE GLASSES

Superior quality Groucho glasses with comfortable rubber nose and larger stems for great fit. Say the secret word and these can be yours! Put them on when you are ready for a humor break. Surprise a relative or co-worker with a visit from Groucho. Put them on – relax and have a good time. Look at life through some silly glasses.

$1.50 each
Buy more and SAVE
5 for $6.50
50 for $60.00

SMILE ON A STICK

Terrific for parties, meetings, events, special occasions and celebrations. Stick a few in a flower arrangement or gift basket. Use them as party invitations or favors. Stick one on top of a present instead of a bow. If they won't give you a smile give them one of yours! Choose from: Original Smile, Multi Cultural, Romance, Clown n' Around, Skull, Jack O'Lantern or Santa on a Stick.

$2.00 each
Buy more and SAVE
Set of 5 $8.50
Set of 50 $82.00

2" RED FOAM CLOWN NOSE

You can pick your friends, you can pick your nose and now you can pick your friend a nose! Wear one to the hospital to cheer someone up. Put one on to change the pace at the office or wear one when you're stuck in traffic to ease the stress. Great for weddings, parties, meeting starters and holidays. Everyone loves a clown! One size fits all.

$1.00 each
Buy more and SAVE
Set of 12 $8.50
Set of 50 $34.00

2" SQUEEZE SMILE BALL

Keep this sunny smile around to remind you to keep the kid in you alive. Doubles as a stress ball. Keep them on your desk, in the kitchen or in the car. When you need a reminder to keep the fun in the dysfunctional or the silly in the stressful, this little smile ball will do the trick. Great in gift bags or in registration packets at conferences.

$1.00 each
Buy more and SAVE
Set of 12 $8.50
Set of 50 $34.00

"There's a very fine line between a groove and a rut; a fine line between eccentrics and people who are just plain nuts."
- Christine Lavin

ABOUT THE AUTHOR

Yvonne Conte is founder and Director of Fun at Crack-A-Smile Seminars. She is a highly sought after and nationally recognized professional speaker, seminar facilitator and the creator of Crack-A-Smile's corporate seminars.

A motivational speaker for business, civic and church groups on a variety of topics, Yvonne's fast paced humorous presentations are peppered with personal anecdotes and real life experience. She provides insights into the trials and triumphs we face at home and in the workplace. Yvonne has met personal challenges, major career changes, death, illness, divorce and single parenthood with unshakable optimism, deep faith, and a sense of humor. She brings laughter and encouragement, delighting her audiences as she offers life-changing material.

Yvonne is the author of Serious Laughter, a guide for living a happier, healthier, more productive life, appeared as a humor consultant on NBC's Syracuse affiliate WSTM's Noon News with Laura Hand.

As a writer and motivational humorist, Yvonne inspires audiences nationally and appeared as a guest on ABC TV's Vicki Lawrence show and on the Caryl and Marilyn Show.

Her children's book, Frankie Wonders...What Happened Today?, is a look at the events of September 11th through a child's eye. This touching book has brought praise from teachers, psychologists, children and parents. All the profits from this book are donated to The Children's Aid Society of New York City.

Yvonne has combined her experience as a comedian, with skills from her fifteen years as an award winning sales executive and introduced her Humor Seminars to the marketplace. Over 25,000 participants in the United States & Canada have attended her presentations. Her highly acclaimed Positive Power of Humor seminar has been called the most powerful & attractive seminar available today.

Love like you've never been hurt.

Dance like nobody's watching.

Sing like nobody's listening.

Live like it's Heaven on Earth.